The Complete

ost
Person
oems

Mark Young

Sandy Press

The Complete Post Person Poems by Mark Young

ISBN: 979-8-9898666-9-4

Cover preparation & design
by harry k stammer

These poems have previously appeared,
sometimes in different versions, in
A New Ulster, dadakuku, Synchronized Chaos,
The Saturday Paper, & on the
gamma ways, mark young's Series Magritte,
& *pelican dreaming* blog sites.

Sandy Press
California
https://sandy-press.com/

sandypress2021@gmail.com

The Complete

ost
P
erson
oems

Today the
postman brought
me the roll of
the coalition
casualties
in Iraq. No lists;
each name a
separate letter. I
complained about
the amount
of mail. "Consider
yourself lucky"
said the postman.
"The couple next
door got the
Iraqis. It took
two trucks to
deliver it all."

Today the
postman brought
me the latest
issue of
Conspiracy Theory Quarterly
in its plain
alfoil wrapper. I
waved to the
satellite as
I carried it in.

Today the
postman brought
me a copy
of *Ulysses*. I
was dis-
appointed. Had
asked for the
Achilles doll.

Today the
postman brought
me a blow-up
sex doll &
a torch. I spent
the night in
shining amour.

Today the
postman brought
me *Scheherazade*. If
you want to find out
what happened then
you're going to
have to wait
until tomorrow.

Today the
postman brought
me John Cage's
X, writings
'79-'82. I went
to sign my
name. "Already
done," he said. "Seen
one **X**, seen them
all." I watched
the postman until
he went around
the corner. Took
him four minutes
& thirty-three
seconds. I stood
silent. He kept
whistling.

Today the
postman brought
me the packet of
instant water
I'd sent away
for four weeks
ago. Nothing
in it except
a two line
instruction.
Just add
water. Stir.

Today the
postman brought
me a postcard
of Venice, sent
by one of the
pelicans that
usually lives
on the lagoon
down the bottom
of the street.
"Strange to be
fishing through
a culture
that's only a few
thousand years
old," she wrote. "But
easy to see how
the Europeans
managed to fuck
Australia over in
just a couple of
centuries after we'd
looked after it for
60,000 years. Look at
this place. Effluent
in the lagoon, dead
fish, houses
in decay or sinking
below the water-
line. Gone to the
doges, as the locals
say. Still, it's great
to be a cultural
nomad for a
while. Paris

last week, the
Greek Isles next. Now
& again I have to
pinch myself, just
to make sure I'm
not dreaming."

Today the
postman brought
me a book on
fundament-
alism. It was
full of assholes,
of all religions.

Today the
postman brought
me an Escher
drawing of the
postman bringing me
an Escher drawing
of the postman
bringing me an
Escher drawing of
the postman
bringing....Five
hours later I
worked out why
I like Magritte.

Today the
postman brought
me the Lone
Ranger & Tonto. Ex-
cept the Lone Ranger
is now no longer
alone because
he is in touch
with his inner self
& Tonto is a psychic
from the sub-
continent & not a
Native American
sidekick. Damn
these shades of
gray. Whatever
happened to black
& white, even
when / in color?
I blame Alan Ladd,
playing Shane with
a small man
syndrome. & Gary
Cooper, the tall
silent one who
learnt to talk &
went off to mix it
with the likes of
Picasso. Wasn't a
virgin Quaker bride
enough for him? You
could see it coming
as it neared high
noon. The hero as
a man in black. Do not

forsake me, I begged
him. Obviously
he didn't listen.

Today the
postman brought
me a laptop
that is claimed
will work under
water. If you're
reading this then
apparently it
does. Un-
fortunately
I don't.

Today the
postman brought
me a digitally
remastered & re-
mixed live
recording of
the Big Bang. For
my tastes it's
a little over-
mined. No
matter.

Today the
postman brought
me the mummified
remains of
André Breton. "You
must have been a
beautiful baby" I
sang as I un-
wrapped them
"'cause baby take
a look at you
now." Such an
exquisite corpse.
"When you were
only starting to
go to kindergarten
I bet you drove the
little boys wild."

Today the
postman brought
me Ernest
Hemingway. I
didn't know
what to do
with him, so
I gave him a
shotgun &
told him to
go off & pretend
he was fighting
bulls or some-
thing. A bit of
noise at first,
but he's been
quiet for the
last few hours.

Today the
postman brought
me a letter from
the City Council
asking residents
in our area
not to dispose of
their colostomy bags
down the toilet.

Apparently they
block the local
pumping station
& cause the sewer-
age to overflow.

How prosaic. I
much preferred
believing it was
the perfume of
night-blooming
asphodels that
had filled the air.

Today the
postman brought
me the new book
by George
W. Bush. It's
Homeric in
both text &
title — text
by Homer Simpson;
title, *I lied*.

Today the
postman brought
me letters
for the Light
Brigade. *They've
moved* I told
him. *Half a
league onward*.

Today the
postman brought
me a man-
dolin that
was ripe
for the
plucking.

Today the
postman brought
me some
freshly layed
aubergines.

Today the
postman brought
me a blow-
up sex doll
which, it is
claimed, can be
   programmed
to become moist
whenever a
music of the
user's choosing
is played. I tried
it out with the
pipes & drums
of the Southern
Highlanders. It
worked. Un-
fortunately
   it didn't
work for me.

Today the
postman brought
me the missing
arms of the Venus
de Milo. I am
using one to write
this note. It
works well, but has
a tendency to
bring out the
softer side of
me. Though possibly
that's because I'm
using the left
where normally
I am right-handed.

Today the
postman brought
me a letter
addressed to
the person who
lived here be
fore me. We
share the same
name. I don't
recognize it.

Today the
postman brought
me a book &
a letter. Sent
two weeks apart;
but in one of
those acts
of synchronicity
that define the
universe they
arrived together. A
review copy of
Donald Rumsfeld's *The*
Deportment of Defense
or *why I'll never*
fall on my sword
in which, in his
own write, he
channels everyone from
Shakespeare — there
are more weapons of
mass destruction in
Iraq, Colin Powell, than
are dreamt of in your
philosophy — to the
Marx Brothers — we
know there are some
things we do not
know. But there are also
unknown unknowns, the
ones we don't know
we don't know. The letter
was from his publisher,
priority-paid, saying
that, because of un-

foreseen circumstances,
the book was now
withdrawn, as was
its author, & could I
return or destroy
it. Fat chance. eBay
beckons for bell,
book, & candle.

Today the
postman brought
me two books
that I had
ordered — *Anger
Management*, &
*How to Overcome
Obsessive Compulsive
Behaviour*. I
punched him up
because he
placed the parcel
in the letterbox
upside-down.

Today the
postman brought
an elephant. I
have no idea
what to do
with it. There
was no instruction
manual included.

Today the
postman brought
a bill
from the glue-
works for
renders
serviced.

Today the
postman brought
me the third
issue of the
series *Patterns
of War*. This is
the one I
have been waiting
for. It shows me
how to knit
a hand-held
missile launcher.

Today the
postman brought
me the riddle
of the Sphinx.
A little later
Oedipus came
along delivering
give-aways. I poked
his eyes out
to save him
future grief.

This afternoon
the postman
called again, a
special delivery
letter. From
Sigmund Freud's
solicitors, informing
me that the
not-yet-great man
was suing me
for blackening
his future fame.

Today the
postman brought
me the new
album by
Charlie
Parker. Jesus.
How do these
dead guys
do it?

Today the
postman brought
me a haiku
from Issa.

Under the
new anti-
terror
legislation
it had to be
translated into
English before
delivery.

Nineteen syllables
in literal translation.
Excess postage was charged.

Today the
postman brought
me a delicate
blue & white
porcelain
vase. *Ming,*
I thought
as I gently
flicked a
fingernail
against the
rim. *Qing,*
it replied.

Today the
postman brought
me several
vials of
frozen bull semen
& the complete
sheetmusic
of John Philip
Sousa. It is
my retirement
dream. The
first Minotaur
Marching
Band.

Today the
postman brought
me the silver
apples of
the moon, the
golden apples
of the sun.

Moments later
the Federal Police
arrived with
the bomb squad
in tow. I was
taken into
custody, the apples
were exploded.
Time's done.

Today the
postman brought
me a book
of word
spells. I
read it. I am
enchanted.

Today the
postman brought
me a tall
ship &
a GPS receiver
to steer
it by.

Today the
postman brought
me a poster-
size portrait
of Terence Stamp
in his role as
Billy Budd. I've
hung it from
the yard-arm.

Today the
postman brought
me a 12" black
disk with a
hole in the
middle. Is
this a record?

Today the
postman brought
me a cello. Sup-
posedly a gift
but there were
strings attached.

Today the
postman brought
me the snows
of yesteryear
but they had
melted before
they got to me.

Today the
postman brought
me an
invitation from
Torquemada
to attend the
Inquisition. Specified
dress. Either
full Inquistorial regalia &
bring a bag or
sackcloth & ashes
& come as you
are. That's the trouble
since Dubya assumed
the Papacy. No
middle of the road
to walk down
anymore.

Today the
postman brought
me a pool of
water from the
Icicle Factory.

Today the
postman brought
me details of
a competition
that simply
involved
using the words
gemütlich &
caoutchouc
in the same poem.
I couldn't think
of any way
to do it so
decided
not to enter.

Today the
postman brought
me The Second
Coming of The
Lord. I found it
impossible to
    swallow. Just
like the first.

Last week the
postman brought
me a letter
from The Church
of The Over-
looked Epilog
saying that, once I
gave my consent,
I would be
canonized on
the basis of
the miracles
my poetry
had wrought. They
gave chapter &
verse — verse
anyway. How
one of my poems
recited incessantly
for seven days
& seven nights
had fended off a
plague of locusts
in Sub-Saharan
Africa. How another,
printed out & mixed
with myrrh & hairgel,
was efficacious as
a cure for river
blindess. How a
third, carried inside
a Tefillin, caused
a stillbirth to be
reversed. I didn't
recognize the titles

of any of the poems
mentioned; but my
memory's not all
it used to be, so
gave my consent
anyway. A sainthood
seemed much more
attractive than the
missing Marcos millions,
discount pharmaceuticals,
superceded software,
or having my cock
elongatedededededededededed
& / or
enlarged.

Today the
postman brought
me an invoice for
$50,000. Plus tax.

Today the
postman brought
me the news
that George
Washington
had died from
hypothermia
whilst attempting
a night time
crossing of
the Delaware.

Today the
postman brought
me my Golden
Globe for best
poetry soundtrack
to an animated
daguerreotype
adapted from a
stage musical or
a foreign-language
reality show.

Today the
postman brought
me a style
    manual. I
opened it up &
picked out a
couple of boxed
heading hierarchies
coated in
dark chocolate to
have with my
morning coffee.

Today the
postman also
brought me
Tolstoy's master-
piece annotated
by the Shrub. I
couldn't get past
the title page —

WAR AND ~~PEACE~~
MORE WAR

Today the
postman brought
me sixteen
Roman Catholic
priests. I'm going
to have to post-
pone services. I need
another five for
a critical mass.

Today the
postman brought
me 101 things
you always
wanted to know
about yourself. At
least I thought
I did, until I
read the thing
about the
serial killer
inside us all.

Today the
postman almost
brought me
a copy of
Proust's *À*
la recherche
du temps perdu.
I found him

asleep on his
motorcycle
a few
doors down
the street
from us.

Today the
postman brought
me a gift-
wrapped camel. I
invited it in for
tea. "One hump
or two?" I asked.

Today the
postman brought
me a letter from
Geof Huth. I'm
still trying
to work out
what fucking
alphabet it
came from.

Today the
postman brought
me "Ventriloquism
for Dummies."

Today
the postman
brought me some

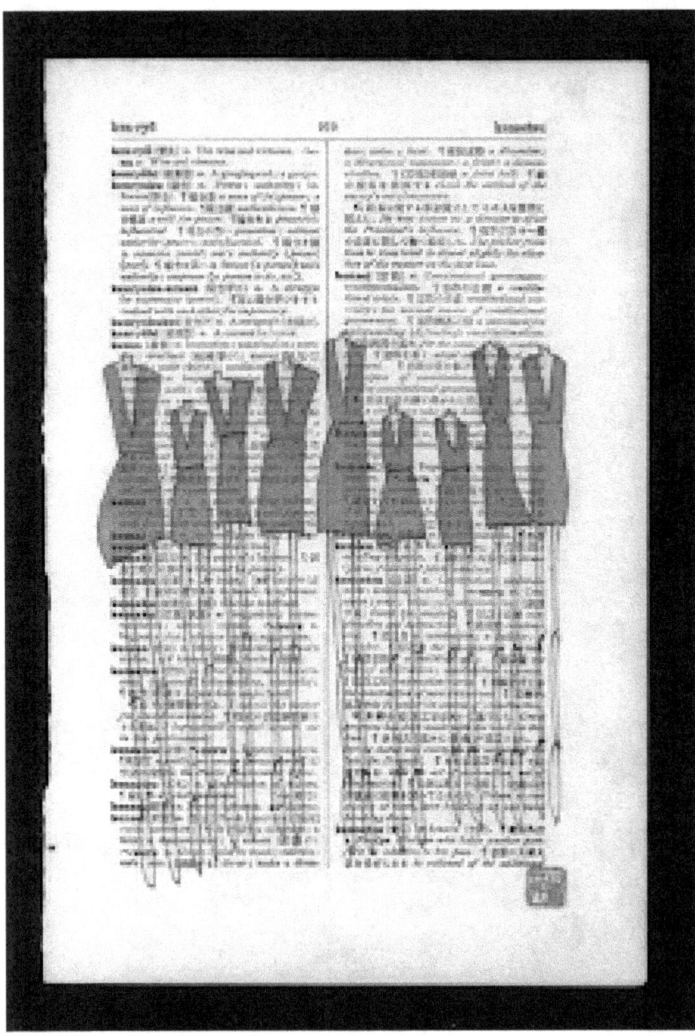

wonderful

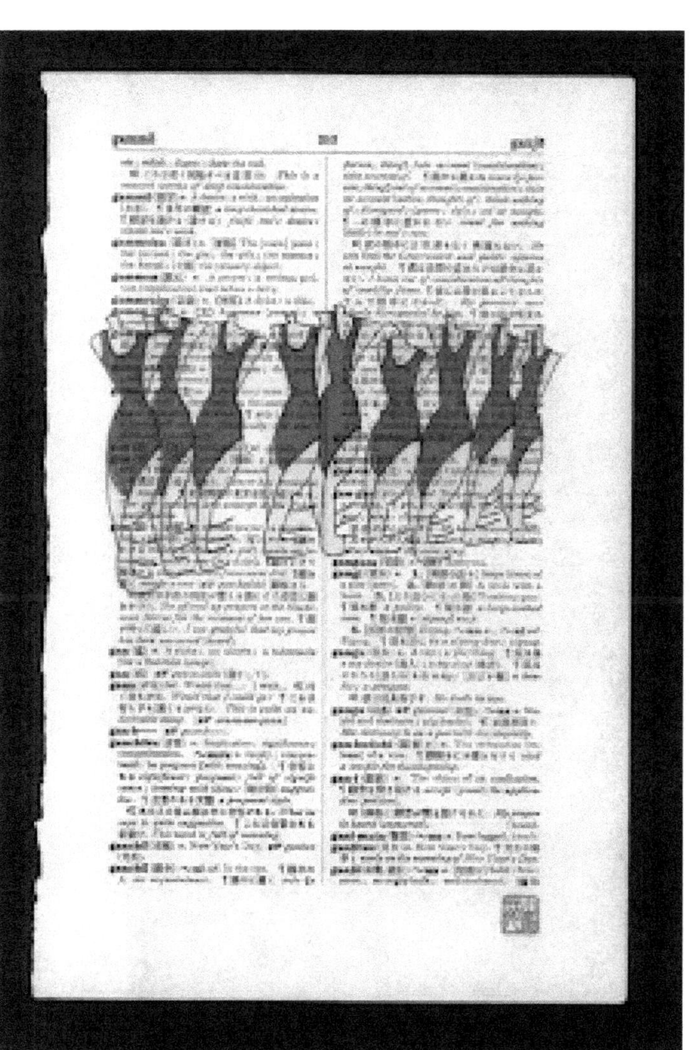

Kabuki Dancers

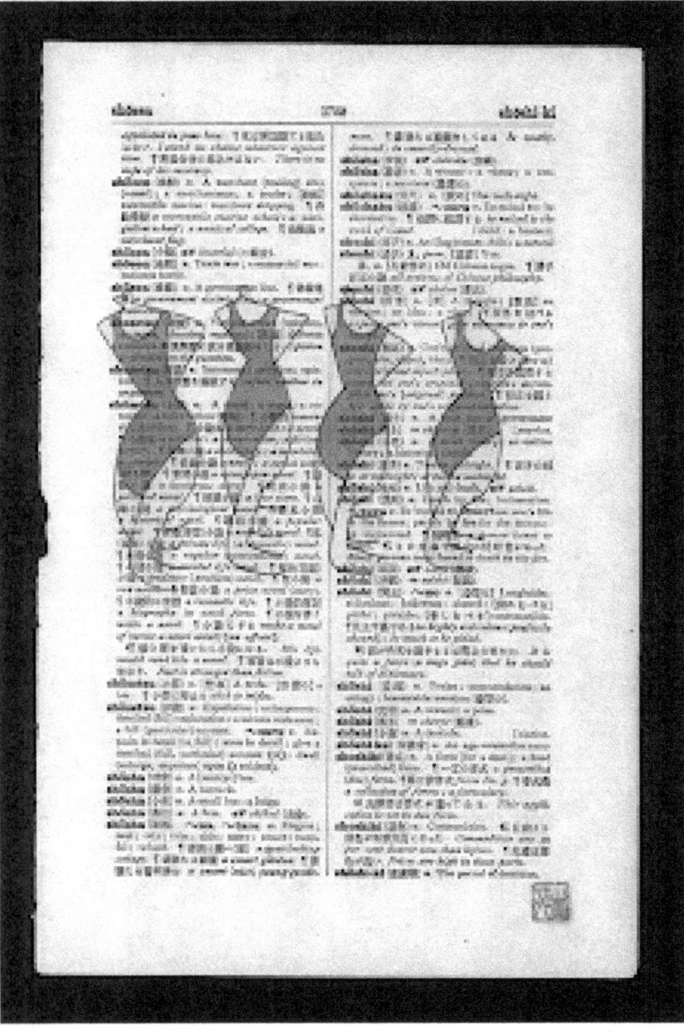

from Ray Craig.

Full-
sized, &
glossy. & in

an
act of
surprising consideration, that

perhaps
shows that
he knows I

talk
about him
behind his back,

the
postman parked
his putput motorcycle

by
the post-
box & walked

down
the path
to leave the

envelope
on the
porch bench so

the
prints inside
would not get

crumpled
or damaged
in any way.

Today the
postman brought
me a delegation
of NeoCon-
servatives. Be
careful with them,
he said, they tend
to drift. The last
lot I delivered
moved so far to
the right they
fell off the
edge of the Earth.

Today the
postman brought
me a suicide-
bomber's vest. "That's
too heavy for this
climate," I told
him. "Do you
have one in string?"

Today the
postman brought
me the can
of worms
I'd always
wanted to open.

Today the
postman brought
me the Swiss Cheese
calendar for 2014.
I've sent it back
because it was
full of holes.

Today the
postman brought
me a book out-
lining the new
stringent
legislation on
Gunk Control. Such
a pity that plumbers,
mechanics, & the
environmental
lobby don't have
the political clout
to nullify the
influence of
the National
Rifle Association.

Today the
postman brought
me a new
edition of *The
Selected Works of
Sigmund Freud*. It's
full of what
appear at first glance
typos—though on
reflection perhaps
deliberate. Esp. when
you find such lines as
".....he dreamt his
mother fucked
him into bed."

Today the
postman brought
me K'ung Fu-
Tse. He’s
supposed to be
from Scotland,
just like me, but
I canna ken
the wee mon’s
funny analect.

Today the
postman brought
me a kilo of
blow. I snorted
in disbelief.

Today the
postman brought
me a little
book by
Geof Huth. It
was totally
Out of Characters.
I love it.

Today the
postman brought
me a kilo of
feathers & a
kilo of lead. He
wants an answer
by tomorrow.

Today the
postman brought
me personalized
letters from
Barbra Streisand
offering me her
complete recordings
in the one boxed
set & from Dr Jack
Kevorkian who is
flogging his "Makes
The Difference" Engine
at just-got-out-of-
prison prices. I
did not respond
to either; but have
used the incident
in my new paper
on Cause & Effect.

Today the
postman brought
me the last
episode of Marcel
Marceau. Finally
he's all mime.

Today the
postman brought
me the terror-
rising news
that the Thought
Police are alive
& well & living
in Australia. The
smallest thing, not
even tangible.....

Today the
postman brought
me the periodic
table to go
with the other
periodic furniture
we have around
the house.

Today the
postman brought
me my
contributor's copy
of *Haiku by
Serial Killers*. It's
the first in a
number of
volumes. The
subsequent
ones will be
published at
ever-decreasing
intervals.

Today the
postman brought
me an optical
allusion & some
special spectacles
to help me
understand it.

Today the
postman brought
me a *Refutation of
Chaos Theory*. I'm
a bit skeptical
about the research,
however, since the
paper opens with
a disclaimer that
no butterflies
were harmed
during the course
of the study.

Today the
postman brought
me a poem that
was written
tomorrow.

Today the
postman brought
me a compendium
of words &
phrases that are
rarely used these
days. Gadzooks!

Today the
postman brought
me the final
volume of *The
Never-Ending
Story*.

Today the
postman brought
me *Larousse
Gastronomique*. I
couldn't get
through it all
in the one
sitting, have put
the leftovers
in the freezer.

Today the
postman brought
me a poem that
he'd stolen
from the
postman
who had stolen
it from Pablo
Neruda. Let me
count the ways.

Today the
postman brought
me a notice from
the Harry Houdini
Trick, Tract, &
Prestidigitation
Emporium
advising that a
number of its
products were
being recalled
because of faulty
mirrors. Many
magicians will be
disillusioned.

Today the
postman brought
me an enquiry
from Schade &
Freud(e)
wondering how
my ego was
now it's been
downgraded
from super-
model status.

Today the
postman brought
me a small
block of granite
entitled *Homage
to Catatonia*. It
is an erased
version of Orwell's
memoir of the
Spanish Civil War.

Today the
postman brought
me the generic
Prozac I'd
ordered from
an online Canadian
Pharmaceutical
company. Not
worth the wait. Some
time back turned my-
self inside out to
hide the blemishes &
make in(tro)spection
easy; & these
pills don't work
when it's surface
tension that needs
to be treated.

Today the
postman brought
me The Tell-
tale Heart. I've
hidden it under
the floorboards.

Today the
postman brought
me a plan
for immediate
world domination. I
wasn't home & the
parcel was too
big to fit in
the letter-box. Now
I have to pick it
up from the
Post Office
some time after
9 a.m. on Monday.

Today the
postman brought
me a *catalogue*
raisonné of
found objects. The
catalog was in-
cluded in the
catalog. Gödel
wouldn't have been
happy about
that inclusion.

Today the
postman brought
me a vortex
on a special
try-before-you-
buy offer. I
got sucked in.

Today the
postman brought
me a carrot on
a stick. I said
neigh to it.

Today the
postman brought
me a flamenco
dancer. Some-
thing clicked
between us—
her castanets.

Today the
postman brought
me the two
Democrat
Presidential
hopefuls. I've
set up a
lockedsteelcagefighttothedeath
match for them,
penciled in a
couple of months
away. Have
borrowed from
the Mexicans &
they'll both have
masks on. That way
the winner won't be
identifiable until the
victorious one exits
the cage & un-
masks themself.

Today the
postman brought
me a mid-
life crisis
& a Ferrari
in a color that
matched my
blood's hot eyes.

Today the
postman brought
me Tom
Beckett. Too
tall to fit
through the
door so I've
left his physical
self outside
as a kind of
toTom pole
& let his
spirit run
free to keep
me company.

Today the
postman brought
me a canteloupe
for my vege-
tarian zoo.

Today the
postman brought
me some
pigeons. Sad-
ly, I no longer
have a cat
to set a-
mongst them.

Today the
postman brought
me the kingdom
of the blind. It's
from a club
I recently joined,
& it's my turn
to be King
for a day.

Today the
postman brought
me a hermetically-
sealed box of
greenhouse gas
emissions. It was
from Macbeth. The
accompanying
note began "Now
Me Thane of Cordor......"

Today the
postman brought
me a prose-
lytizer but I
can't seem
to make
it work.

Today the
postman brought
me a *leporidae*
farm. It had
been beautifully
maintained,
not a hare
out of place.

Today the
postman brought
me a brochure
from Monsanto
that claims the
use of genetically-

modified crops
will break
the cycle of
poetry that is
endemic in
some third world

countries. Should
that happen, I
see the entire
world being
a poorer place
& oh so prosaic.

Today the
postman brought
me a magnetized
calendar from
the local personal
injury litigation
lawyers. It was
the only mail; &,
smaller than a
regular envelope,
didn't stay
protruding from
the aperture
but slid quickly
into the depths
of the mailbox
where it severed
the tail of the
little brown gecko
that lives there. Con-
fronted by the
conjunction of a
separated piece
of itself & "Have
you been in an
accident recently?"
the gecko has de-
cided to sue the
singer & pursue the
song, has ordered
legal textbooks from
Amazon to prepare
its case. Didn't care
what books they
sent; just asked

that they be too big
to fit in a mailbox.

Today the
postman brought
me the fifteen
nanoseconds
of fame allotted
me under the
latest Free
Trade agree-
ment. I
blinked &
missed it.

Today the
postman brought
me a horse de-
signed by a
committee. They
call it a camel.

Today the
postman brought
me a blow up
Sarah Palin
doll. Oops,
I'd better add
a hyphen be-
fore the postman
brings me Home-
land Security.

Today the
postman brought
me a giant
squid from
20,000 leagues
beneath the
sea. I was so
looking for-
ward to having
battered jumbo
calamari rings
for dinner but
it didn't survive
the journey, &
squid soup
just doesn't
cut it somehow.

Today the
postman brought
me a letter from
Leonardo da
Vinci. I had
to reflect on it
for quite some
time before
I was able to
draft a reply. I'll
be so glad when
he gets around
to getting an
email account.

Today the
postman brought
me a piano
accordion. I
don't know what
I've done to
make him
hate me so.

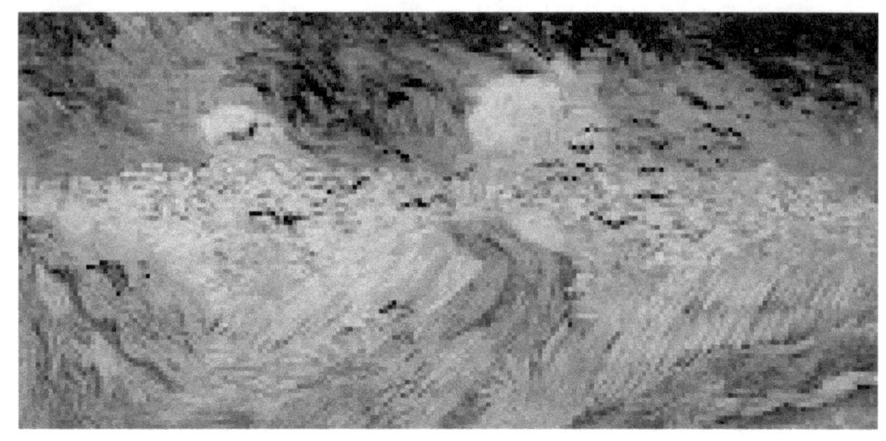

Today the
postman brought
me an invitation
to nominate
my favorite
Impressionist
painting. What to
pick? I've been
weighing up the
crows & ponds.

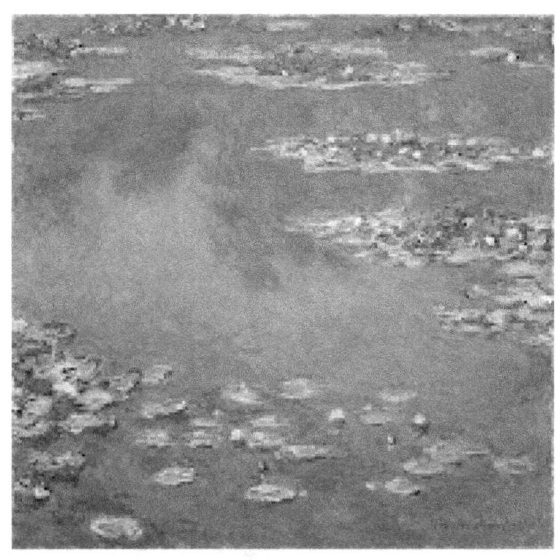

Today the
postman brought
me a large Bo
tree. I have re-
planted it in
the overgrown
back garden be-
tween the lychee
& the macadamia.

Next week I am
going for a
holiday, & there
will be no-one
here to hear it
if it falls. Will
Buddha-mind?

Today the
postman brought
me the de-
nominator I
needed to
traverse the
Great Divide.

Today the
postman brought
me the Grand
Canyon. Not
the walls: just
the space within,
deflated to make
for cheaper
shipping. It's
funny. I always
thought it
would be bigger.

Today the
postman brought
me a tracking
cookie. I don't
mind it
following me
around the
house, but I
hate the crumbs
it leaves behind.

Today the
postman brought
me a fake
Louis Vuitton
suitcase inside
of which was a
real & very rotten
sheep carcass. God I
hate those overseas
call centers! This
wasn't what I had
in mind when I
rang the number
on the screen
to order a set of
carry-on luggage.

Today the
postman brought
me a bridge. I'm
waiting for my
ship to come in
so I can open it.

Today the
postman brought
me the Time-Life
extraordinary renditions
selection I'd written
away for. The
package was
larger than I'd
expected; some
kind of mistake
had been made. What
do razorwire, hooded
prisoners, & torture
cells have to do
with Great Arias
from Great Operas
by Great Sopranos?

Today the
postman brought
me the Shield
of Achilles. So
much mystique
attached to it
that, upon re-
flection, I
was petrified.

Today the
postman brought
me some fragments
from the in-
complete skeleton
of *Pithecanthropus*
erectus. I ground
them up, in-
fused them in
liquid to see
if I could isolate
some DNA. A
succesful ex-
periment—I always
did make a good
cup of Java.

Today the
postman brought
me a bath
that had been
thrown out
with the
babywater.

Today the
postman brought
me the macaw
I'd ordered
off the internet.
Caveat emptor—
I got sent a
Scottish crow.

Today the
postman brought
me a square
peg & a
square hole. It's
a kind of
security blanket.

Today the
postman brought
me the riddle
of the Sphinx. I
walked out to
get it; but on
the way back
tripped on the
packing tape
which had come
unwrapped in
transit & had
to crawl like a
baby the rest
of the way. The
ankle wasn't
broken, just
sprained; but I'm
using a walking
stick to get around
for the next few
days. Feeling fine
otherwise. Now
what was the
question again?

Today the
postman brought
me a grassy
knoll & a Presi-
dential motor-
cade. Now
all I need
is a fall guy.

Today the
postman brought
me *jambandbootleg*
by Paul Seigell. &,
hand-written on
the back of the
envelope, a poem
from the author:
"Today the
postman brought
me *jambandbootleg*
by Paul Seigell."
It took the words
right out of my
mouth. Meatloaf
& PHiSH. *Quel
combination!* I'd
like to see that.

Today the
postman brought
me a satellite
navigation
system with
Bob Dylan
doing the voice-
overs. Worked
fine until we
were coming
up to Highway
61. Then it
stopped giving
directions &
started asking
"where do I
want the
killings done?"

Today the
postman brought
me *Indiana
Jones & The
Walking Frame.*

Today the
postman brought
me a postcard
from André
Breton who
writes that he
is alive &
well, & co-
habiting with
an abandoned
kaleidoscope
off the coast
of Costa Rica.

Today the
postman brought
me three
of the four
humors. "Sorry
about the
missing one,"
he said,
phlegmatically.

Today the
postman brought
me the Noble
Piece Prize plus
a sac(k)full of
endorsement
requests from
the many
penis enlargement
companies I've
dealt with
over the years.

Today the
postman brought
me the *catalogue
raisonné* of a
Flemish Master
who doesn't
yet exist. I've
conceptualized
his creations
with the names
that are listed in
the catalog. I'm
still working on
his creation, am
using that fictional
detective from
Los Angeles as
his working name.

a found postman poem

Yesterday I
ordered the
lightweight
tranny parts off
monster garage, &

today the
postman brought
me my dirt-
bones—they look
beast—& my
novarace head
which is a very
nice piece of
machining. Now I
just need my wasp
for it to go on.

Today the
postman brought
me soap on a
rope, the Pope
on dope, hope
on a slope, a
trope at a lope.
I couldn't cope.

"Don't bring
the ingredients
next time," I
told him. "Just
the finished
Dr Seuss book."

Today the
postman brought
me de Sade's
120 Days of
Sodom. It has
a 30-day
money-back
guarantee.

Today the
postman brought
me an invitation
to the opening
of the latest
in a chain of
goodwill stores
all filled with
what used
to be directed
towards the
President.

Today the
postman brought
me a fart
in a jar. Damn
that voice re-
cognition
software—
I'd asked for
a jam tart
to go with my
morning coffee.

Today the
postman brought
me a book en-
titled *What is
Peripheral
Vision*. I didn't
see him come
into view.

Today the
postman brought
me a calliope. He
was all steamed
up about it. So,
too, the calliope.
Instant (re)play.

Today the
postman brought
me a box of
Girl Scout
tracking cookies.

Truly a corn-
ucopia. Tomorrow
he'll be back
with another box
containing much
the same as
those I've
just consumed.

Today the
postman brought
me a Buddhist's
lament

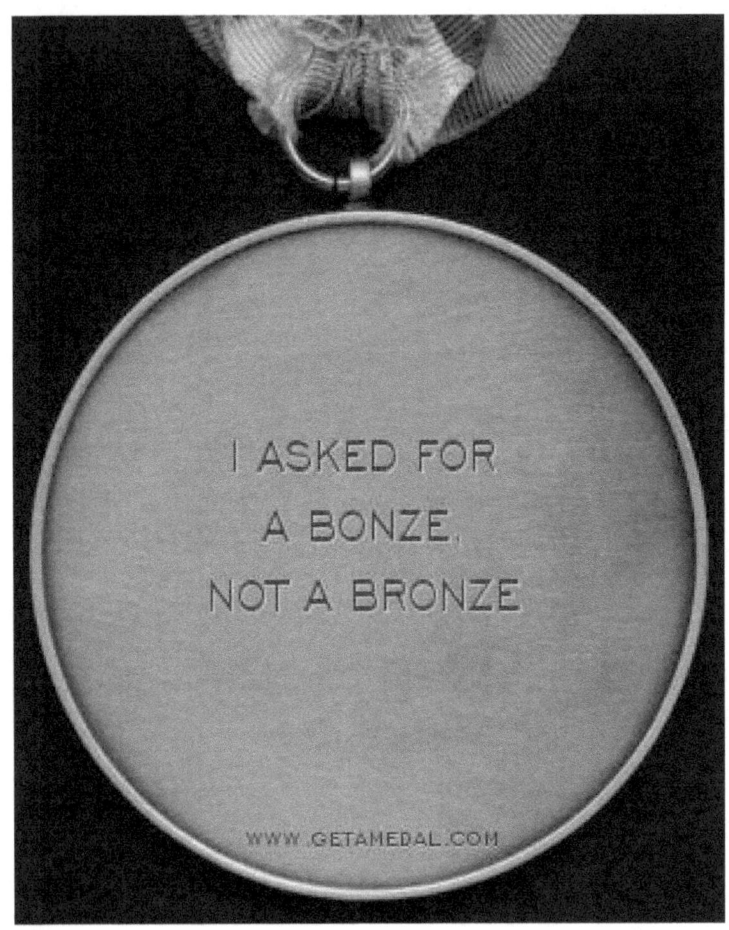

Today the
postman brought
me a concrete
poem. Just two

quatrains: but
still needed
both of us to
carry it inside.

Today the
postman brought
me *The Shorter
Oxford English
Dictionary*. Such
generosity! I was
lost for words.

Today the
postman brought
me *Fundamental
Humor*. Mis-
representation if
you ask me. Not
a fart joke in it.

Today the
postman brought
me a seven-figure
check in payment
for the piece of
thick artist's paper
I'd left under the
front door mat
for six months &
then sold on eBay
as the original
Rauschenburg
erasure of de
Kooning's nude.

I'm a little bit
worried though.
Modern technology
being what it is
it won't be long
before what I
described as the
vestigial remnants
of the figure are
identified as a
not-too-clear
impression of
the maker's mark,
an image of Kali
& beneath it:

The
Bengali
Coir Mat
Factories
P/L.

Today the
postman brought
me nothing. An
empty mailbox
later filled by a
green & yellow
tree snake
which watched
silently as I de-
toured around it
taking the garbage
out. That arc re-
traced returning
until eye contact
broken. Which
is when the
snake spoke. Said:
"What does not change /
is the will to change."

Today the
postman brought
me a book on
plagiarism. No-
thing I hadn't
read before,
word for word,
in a number
of other books.

Today the
postman brought
me the letters
W & S. We
watched *Sesame
Street* together.

Today the
postman brought
me an unsigned
ransom note
threatening to
destroy the world
unless I came up
& across with $10
million in incon-
sequential bills.
"Such is life," I
thought & threw it
in the garbage. Ex-
istentialism does
have an upside.

Today the
postman brought
me back to
reality.

Today the post-
woman brought
me a sacrificial
pig. Looks
as if lamb, like
most red meat
these days,
is too expensive
to be used as
anything more
than metaphor.

Today the
postman brought
me a compendium
of investigative
studies by Shop-
Wiki & others
that report an
average of 13
people per year
are killed by over-
tipping vending
machines but less
than one every
two years is
killed by under-
tipping a waiter.

Today the
postman brought
me a letter
for Abraham
Lincoln. He's here
only during the
winter months
so I sent it on,
c/o his Gettys-
burg address.

Today the
postman brought
me an Andy
Warhol silk-
screen print of an
Iams Veterinary
Formula Intestinal
Low-Residue Dog
Food can, done
before The Factory,
before fame. De-
tractors call it
his Pup Art phase.

Today the
postman brought
me Babe
Ruth's *Greatest
Hits* & Jane
Austen's
Greatest Misses.

Today the
postman brought
me a pair of
elevator shoes
that took me
straight to the
top floor. Pity
about the
music that
came with them.

Today the
postman brought
me next week's
lottery numbers—
one through to
forty-four, the
same as this,
last, & every
week for the
past ten years.

Today the
postman brought
me a walking
stick. Now all I
need are a back
fence & a fruit-
filled apple tree
just inside it but
not too far out
of reach for the
young kids of
the neighbor-
hood. Those who
can remember
the past are also
condemned to re-
peat it. I never did
like Santayana.

Today the
postman brought
me a glass
ceiling. Not
for me, I told
him. Perhaps
for the lady
next door.

Today the
postman brought
me my contributor's
copy of

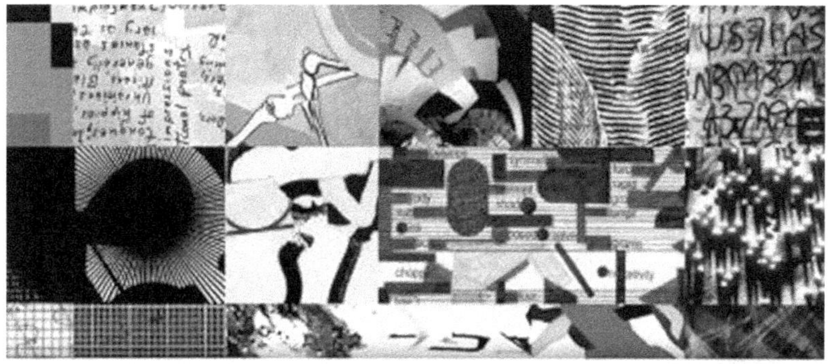

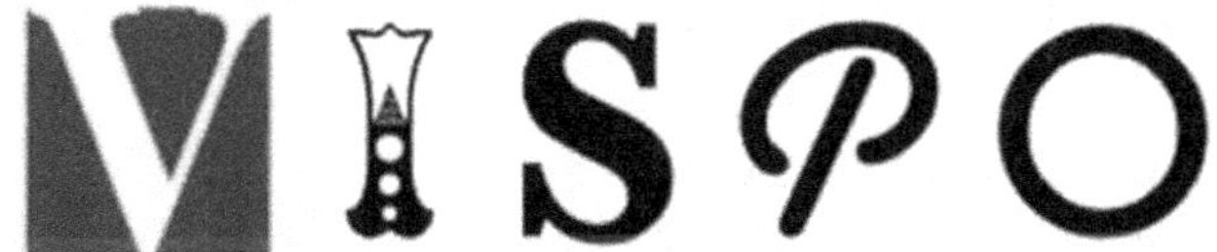

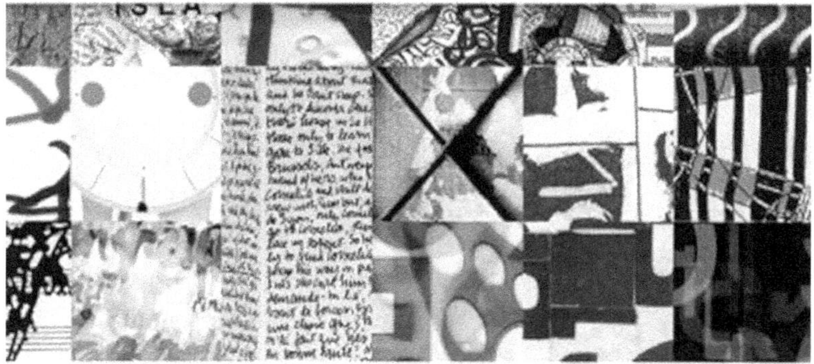

So long
in the making, so
worth the wait.

Today the
postman brought
me the candelabrum
famous for
playing *A Song*
to Remember on
a grand piano
& on top of which
first Chopin &
then, later,
Liberace sat.

Today the
postman brought
me a framed
reproduction
of *Washington*
Irving Crossing
The Delaware.
"What's wrong
with the pict-
ure?" he asked
when I questioned
its provenance.

Six found postman poems

Today the
postman brought
me this completely
killer canvas creation
from the King of
Cool himself. I
fucking love it. Try
not to be too jealous.

Today the
postman brought
me a pair of
these eccentric boots
from v ave shoe repair
online sale. How much
more scandinavian
can you go?

Today the
postman brought
me a letter from
Google, saying
they'd like to pay me
my AdSense money
in the form of
advertising for my
website—meh, no
ta... plain ol' cash
will do, thanks.

Today the
postman brought
me my order from
27th nov. The
pomade has taken
a very long travel.
Now I'm happy
to be able to use
this superb pomade.

Today the
postman brought
me yet another
of your sweet
gifts. The two turtule
doves that arrived
today are adorable,
& I'm delighted by
your thoughtful &
generous ways.

Today the
postman brought
me a proper
letter! With a
hand-written
address!

Today the
postman brought
me what looked
like some sort
of interrogation
technique. I had
to ask him: is this

a glottal stopʔ

Today the
postman brought
me a ticket in
the latest raffle
run by Farmsex.

com where the
first prize is a
poke in a pig
& you get to
choose the pig.

Today the
postman brought
me a mass-mailed—
but individually ad-
dressed & personally
signed in blue ink—
"letter" from the
Postal Service
Director herself
asking me to part-
icipate in an online
survey about min-
imizing fiscal outlay
by reducing mail
deliveries to every
other day of the
week. Today the
postman wore a
black tee on which,
in blue, the message:
morituri te salutant.

Today the
postman brought
me the auto-
biography of a
proofreader,
entitled *My Life
in Correctional
Services.*

Today the
postman brought
me an unemployed
dancing monkey. Put
me down as some-
one who can't tell
a lymph node
from a lung, but I
think there may
currently be a search
on for organ donors.

Today the
postman brought
me the Grand
Mufti of Jeru-
salem. I didn't
recognize him
out of uniform.

Today the
postman brought
me an asteroid
belt. Pity I've
got no suit/able
trousers to
wear it with.

Today the
postman brought
me an aspidistra.
George Orwell
once told me
I had to keep
them flying. I'm
trying, George,
I'm really try-
ing. But it's very
hard to do when
there isn't that
much wind about.

Today the
postman brought
me a bandicoot.

Don't ask.

Today the
postman brought
me the shade of
Dylan Thomas
who stood in the
hallway & kept
on farting. Now I
know what was
meant by that
"when I was a
windy boy" thing
even though he got
the tense wrong.

Today the
postman brought
me a cast iron
alibi. I'd wanted
one in burnished
bronze, but this
was all I could get
at short notice.

Today the
postman brought
me the end
of the world. It
whimpered at
me. Goddamned
Preacher. Spoiled
things for every
pyrotechnician.

Today the
postman brought
me a trickle
down effect, &
the irrigation system
that ensures it.

Today the
postman brought
me the large-print
edition of *Life in
The Fast Lane.*

Today the
postman brought
me a refugee
camp. "What's
this?" I asked
him. "It's the cast-
off thousands you
said you wanted,"
he replied.

Today the
postman brought
me a letter I
had written re-
plying to a letter
I had earlier
written to my-
self. I was so
disappointed to
find nothing
new in it.

Today the
postman brought
me semen from
a papal bull. Un-
fortunately, the
only holy cow
I know of is too
busy camping

it up with the
rest of the crew
of the sixties TV
series *Batman*
to be available
for insemination.

Today the
postman brought
me The City That
Never Sleeps. "I'm
here for some R&R"
it said," & promptly
crashed out on the
La-Z-Boy in the front
room where it's
been snoring for
the last four hours.

Today the postman brought me a Caliphate safe house in Syria. "What's this?" I said. "I asked for an RAF Tornado jet." "Don't worry," said the postman. "I've leaked the co-ordinates. There'll be a bomber along very very soon."

Today the postman brought me a distressed ukelele. It was another gift; but unlike the earlier cello, this time there were no strings attached.

Today the
postman brought
me a package
from the Amelia
Earhart Foundation
in Nigeria purporting
to contain A. E.'s
last words embel-
lished on a vellum
scroll & encased
within a container
made of metal from
the Lockheed Electra
in which she made
her lost last flight.

Today the
postman brought
me a *pièce de*
résistance. Just
the one—I'm
on a diet.

Today the
postman brought
me a Quarter
Pounder™, small
World Famous
Fries™, & a large
Coke™. "I've
delivered you
Civilization™,"
he said.

Today the
postman brought
me a severe
dose of para-
noia. I thought
long & hard
about leaving it
at room temper-
ature, but finally
decided to keep
it chilled until I
could celebrate
people stopping
talking about me.

Today the
postman brought
me a pickle-
odeon. The films
that came with
it were a bit on
the sour side, but I
much preferred
them to the
sweetness other-
wise on offer.

Today the
postman brought
me the fourth
day of Christmas.

Sorry I'm late,
he said, but
it's been a bit
tricky trying to
catch the calling
birds without
animal welfare
getting on my case.

Today the
postman brought
me a nuclear
warhead with a
personal message
from the President
emblazoned on it—
"Hope this launches
your career," it said.
I'd been told his
comprehension skills
weren't all that great;
but thought he'd
understood when I
asked him if he still
intended to launch
a nuclear strike
on North Korea.

Today the
postman brought
me his new
libretto, called
*The Pantoum
of The Opera-
ting Theater*. I
suggested a slight
name change &
a relocation of the
story. "Might work
then," I told him.

Today the
postman brought
me the State of
Denmark. I sent
it back — some-
thing was rotten.

Today the
postman brought
me a directive
from the Secret
Service stating
that their Com-
mander-in-Chief,
because of his re-
fusal to accept the
science of climate
change, would,
in future, have
POTASH as his id-
entifying acronym.

Today the
postman brought
me an abacus.
"Does it still
work?" I asked.
"I wouldn't count
on it," he replied.

Today the
postman brought
me a considered
rebuttal of John
Knox's *The First
Blast of the Trumpet
Against the Monstrous
Regimen of Women*. He
was pleased it was
finally finished,
had taken him
nearly 450 years
to do so. Was dis-
appointed so much
bigotry remained.

Today the
postman brought
me a diktat from
the Governor of
Texas stating
that Hurricane
Harvey was an
act of God in-
telligently de-
signed to either

drive illegal
immigrants out
& onto the high-
ways where they
can be caught by
the Border Patrol
checkpoints—which
will be staying open
for business—or

to keep them in
their homes, too
frightened to risk
venturing out be-
cause of the afore-
mentioned B. P.
personnel, & thus
likely to become
a statistic in two
lists; that of the

dead, & that of
the ever-decreasing
number of paper-

less people still
living in the state.
He closes by saying
how great it is to
see the President's
policies working.

Today the
postman brought
me a bag of beans
& a notice of claim
by the executors
of the estate of
the late Ray Charles,
alleging breach of

copyright by my
using without per-
mission a phrase
from a song he
was the first to
have a hit with.

Today the
postman brought
me a military
parade down
Pennsylvania
Avenue. I was
so disappointed
Where are the
submarines? I
shouted out. *You*
promised you'd
drain the swamp
so I'd be able
to see the submarines
that were lying
on the bottom.

Today the post-
woman brought
me my monthly
credit card state-
ments. "Where's
the other guy?" I
asked her. "Retired
suddenly," she replied.
"Bought himself a
cottage & a block
of land out in the
country. Is going
to raise alpacas
& write his auto-
biography, called, I
believe, *Today the
postman brought
me…*"

Today the post-
woman brought
me a capital
letter. It felt
like a small
case of *déjà vu*.

Today the post-
woman brought
me one of those
so-called smart
bombs. Don't
know why they
call them that. I
asked this one a
couple of simple
questions & it
couldn't answer
either of them.

Today the post-
woman brought
me the ass-end
of Donuts T®ump.
"That wasn't what
I asked for," I told
her. "I wanted to
see the end of that
ass T®ump, not this
crappy T®umped-
up rump."

Today the post-
woman brought
me a slice of
gorgonzola. I ate

it later while
reading *La Bête
humaine* & got
turned to stone.

Today the post-
woman brought
me a broken
promise. "Do
you want that
before or after
the m?" she asked.

Today the post-
woman brought
me a check-
ered board from
Rrose Sélavy.

Today the post-
woman brought
me an empty
envelope
on the back of
which was printed

**THE COMPLETE VERI-
FIABLE SPEECHES
OF DONALD TRUMP.**

Just that, nothing else.

Today the post-
woman brought
me a hula hoop.
It ran rings
around me.

Today the post-
woman brought
me a man who'd
lost his leg to an
alligator. "Which
one?" I asked.
"Can't tell," he
said. "You've seen
one 'gator, you've
seen them all."

Today the post-
woman brought
me a pamphlet
describing the ways
in which erectile
dysfunction can
be a frightening
thing if left un-
treated. It made
me stiff with fear.

Today the post-
woman brought
me an already ex-
pensive castle in
the Pyrenees. If
I had added the

optional extra of
that giant bird
found in some
Magritte paintings
it would have cost
me an arm & a leg

on top of a basic
price I can't really
afford. & since Ma-
gritte is dead, I don't
trust the vendor's
guarantee that the

artist will paint
any missing limbs
back on me, just
like he did to the
model in *Attemp-
ting the Impossible.*

Today the post-
woman brought
me an audio
recording of
the love that
dare not speak
its name.

Today the post-
woman brought
me a ground to air
missile launcher
with black currant &
sweet red capsicum
on the nose & under-
lying subtle smoky
hints of oak
& gooseberry.

Today the post-
woman brought
me a creative
urge. I've sent
it out into the
kitchen to get
dinner ready.

Today the post-
woman brought
me a lifesize full-
color effigy of
Donald Trump. I
put it in the back-
yard to keep the
fruit bats at bay.

The plan backfired.
So much orange
that the fruit bats—
dare I say it?—
went bananas &
have started
arriving in ever-
increasing numbers.

Today the post-
woman brought
me a birthday
card from the
Marquis de
Sade. *Not for
me,* I told her,
*two houses up
the road.* I ran
to retrieve it
the minute she
was out of sight.

Today the post-
woman brought
me a conundrum.
I don't know
what to
make of it.

Today the post-
woman brought
me a candelabra

& a grand piano.
Yet another error
in AI transcription.

I'd asked for a
library of ethics, got
Liberace's effects.

Today the post-
woman brought
me a red Donald
Trump cap. Slightly
different from
the ones you'll
find worn by
the man & his
slavish devotees.

This one addressed
to those outside
the country who
may or may not
remember the Ugly
American of Graham
Greene fame but are
aware of him anyway.

MAKE AMERICA
GRATE AGAIN.

Today the post-
woman brought
me a bacon &
egg burger with
aioli dressing. It
wasn't what I
wanted — I'd
actually asked
for the Gettysburg
Address — but
I didn't complain.
Hunger causes us
to compromise
sometimes.

Today the post-
woman brought
me the plot of
Bambi. She came
empty-handed.

Today the post-
woman brought
me her pandemic
polemic. Stood
1.5 meters away
to argue that

much of the
population was
so confused &
troubled by the
many conflicting
opinions being
bandied around

that a polemic
pandemic would
inevitably break out
& consume the planet
given the eminently
suitable conditions for
exponential growth.

Today the post-
woman brought
me the carapace
of Kara Thrace. I
turned turtle.

Today the post-
woman brought
me a jar of marm-
alade. I looked
at her quizzically.
"Oranges & lemons,"
she said. "It's my day
for delivering nursery
rhymes. You owe
me five farthings."

Today the post-
woman brought

me six *billets-doux,*
five bills of lading,

four biltong sandwiches,
three billowing blouses,

two bilious bandicoots,
& one bilboquet, bowler-

hatted & signed by
René Magritte.

Today the post-
woman brought
me Thelonius
Monk, served as
intended — straight,
no chaser. "Mel-
odious Thunk,"
said Nellie.

Today the post-
woman brought
me a red face
mask with a
White House decal
over the mouth
area. Inside was a
label: *hand-made
by Ivanka Trump
from one of Our
Beloved Leader's
ties*. Delicately em-
broidered around the
bottom border: *Pro-
duct of Bangladesh*.

Today the post-
woman brought
me *le temps
perdu*. I couldn't
remember where
I'd left it, had been
searching for some
time. Turns out I'd
dropped it at the
COVID-testing clinic
on Swann's Way.

Today the post-
woman brought
me the winter
of our discontent,
the Arab spring,
& the summer of
love, as compen-
sation because the
bookshop couldn't
supply my recent
order, *The Fall*, by
Albert Camus.

Today the post-
woman brought
me *L'oiseau de
feu*. It had dust all
over it, made the
postwoman sneeze.

She bent her elbow to
cover her mouth in
the approved COVID
manner. Stra-VINSKY!!

Today the post-
woman brought
me an elephant.
"What's this?" I asked.
"Wondered if you
were interested in a
pet," she replied. "It
was thrown out from
a house earlier on my
round. A big guy
lives there, named
Hannibal. Apparently
he's downsizing after
a trip across the Alps,
& there wasn't room
in the room for both
him & the elephant."

Today the post-
woman brought
me a quart of Old
Grand Dad 114. I'd
actually asked for
a book on the Court
of Bourbon; but the
voice-response soft-
ware must have
interpreted my dulcet
tones as being whis-
keyed rather than quiz
kid, & modified my
request to reflect that.

Today the post-
woman brought
me some ephemera—

at least that's
what the customs
declaration on the

now empty box
said was sup-
posed to be in it.

Today the post-
woman brought me
the new collection
of short poems by
DoNuts T.®ump
entitled *Massive
fraud has been
found*.

A sample example:

> They talk about
> glitches. How many
> glitches did they
> find? Oh, gee, we
> had a glitch, 5000
> votes. We're like a
> third-world country.

The book is
edited by Rudlie
Giulieandlieandlie
& selected copies
are signed in hair-
product by both
RuG & the DTs.

Today the post-
woman brought
me a CD of DoNuts
T.®ump trying
to recite *The Star-
Spangled Banner*
when I'd asked for
a sharp-angled
spanner to be de-
livered. *Why this?*
I asked. *Listen to
the words,* she said.
*I just wanted to point
out to the oft-critical
poet that there's some-
one even more inept
at using the correct
words than I am, &
he used to be the
fucking President.*

Today the post-
woman brought me
Bud Abbott. Who's
on first? I asked him.
He punched me in
the face. He hasn't
been the same since
Lou Costello passed.

Today the post-
woman brought
me a pterodactyl.
I'd actually asked
for some *pommes*
de terre au gratin;
but these days
you take what
you can get, &
are grateful for it.

Today the post-
woman brought
me a split infini-
tive. I ran out to
quickly collect it.

Today the post-
woman brought
me a life-sized
re-enactment of
the first crossing
of the Atlantic
Ocean by a pedal-
powered liferaft. I
almost drowned.

Today the post-
woman brought
me a cartouche.
"What's this?" I
asked.

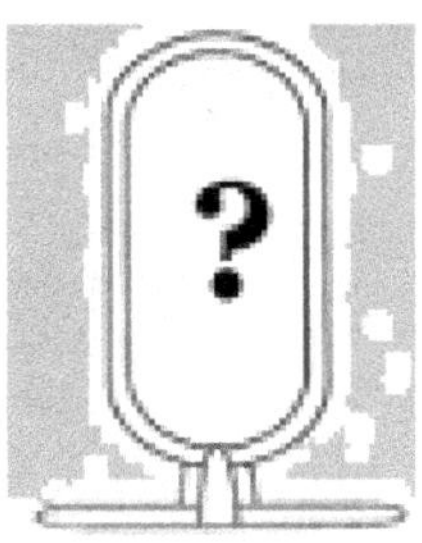

she said.

Today the post-
woman brought
me a brochure
from EARWAX—
extinct animal
resurrection with
academic expertise—
suggesting that if
I donated both
money & a sample
of my DNA they
might be able
to bring back
the Amazonian
smilodon. I de-
clined. Now if it
had have been
the mastodon . . .

Today the post-
woman brought
me Tropical Cy-
clone Kirrily. I
was blown away.

Today the post-
woman brought
me Zeno. I'm try-
ing to get him into

the house in stages,
covering half of
the remaining
distance each time

we move, but we
don't seem able to
get there. Some-
what paradoxical.

Today the post-
woman brought
me the DVD
of Peter Quince
eating caviar
that prompted the
well known poem
by Wallace Stevens.

Today the post-
woman brought

me a manual
on how to write

serious poetry
& not go off

into mad flights
of fancy whenever

a thought settles
like a butterfly

on the leaves
of your tree.

Today the post-
woman brought
me a pasta
maker. My
heart gave out —
I'd asked for
a pacemaker.

Today the post-
woman brought
me a trans-
Atlantic passenger
liner. I tried to

sail it in the lagoon
at the bottom of the
street but when I got
it in there it wouldn't
budge, something to

do with Newton's
unpublished fourth
law of motion which,
in précis, posits big
fish / big pool. I've

decided to leave the
liner where it is,
open it up as
an hotel. The
pelicans are pissed.

Today the post-
woman brought
me the ceiling
of the Sistine

Chapel. Dam-
aged in transit,
so I'm having
it repainted. A

really dark
blue, & then
I'll paste some
stars on it.

Today the post-
woman brought
me a Stillson
wrench. I'm
still trying
to come to
grips with it.

Today the post-
woman brought
me a punching
bag in the like-
ness of Donald
Trump. I'm

thinking about
sending it back.
$a + b - a = b$ —
I've done the
math. If you
knock the shit

out of a shithead
you're left with
just the head. &
who wants to
be left with a
head like that?

Today the post-
woman brought
me two lengths
of pipe. "Right,"
she said, & left.

Today the post-
woman brought
me a walking
frame. I couldn't
keep up with it.

Today the post-
woman brought
me a room to put
the elephant in.

Today the post-
woman brought
me a poem from
William Carlos

Williams. Special
delivery. No letter,
no card. Just the
spoken word.

Stopped her bike
at the top of the
steps & started
to recite in a voice

equally suited for
delivering babies
or poems. "A big
young bareheaded

woman in an apron...."
I was impressed.
Waited until she
had finished &

gave her the flight
of small cheeping
birds that were in
the ice box & which

you were probably
saving for my old age.

Forgive me.

www.ingramcontent.com/pod-product-compliance
Lightning Source LLC
LaVergne TN
LVHW010927110826
845149LV00013B/2506
9798989866694